Disney
FROZEN

Olaf Likes Summer

Level 1

Re-told by: Gregg Schroeder
Series Editor: Rachel Wilson

Before You Read

In This Book

Olaf
the Snowman

Princess
Anna

Queen
Elsa

Activity

**Who lives in a castle? Read
and say Yes or No.**

1 a princess
2 a teacher
3 a queen

It's summer and it's hot today.

This is Olaf. He's happy.
He likes summer.

Anna is in the castle.
It's a beautiful day.

Where is Elsa? There she is!

Do you like lemonade?
Oooo! Yes, I like lemonade!

Olaf, Anna, and Elsa see
flowers and animals.

They see boys and girls.
They run and play in the garden.

Olaf and the sisters go to the beach.
The water is nice and cold.

The sand is nice and hot!

They play on the beach.
There are sand castles.

There is water.
There are birds. Hello, birds!

Now Olaf and the sisters
are hungry. They have lunch.

They go home on the boat.
The colors are beautiful.

Summer is nice.

Hmm ... Elsa likes cold days.

After You Read

1 **Match the words and the pictures.**

1 bird
2 flowers
3 boy and girl
4 happy

2 **Read and say Yes or No.**

1 Olaf likes summer.
2 Elsa, Anna, and Olaf draw and read.
3 They run and play.
4 The water is hot today.
5 The sand is nice.

Picture Dictionary

boat

water

beach

cold

garden

hot

sand castle

sand

summer

Phonics

Say the sounds. Read the words.

L l

lemon

lunch

R r

rice

run

Say the rhyme.

I like lemonade.
I like rice.
Lemonade and rice
For lunch is nice!

Values

Appreciate nature.

What do you do at the beach?

We make sand castles.
We play in the water.
We see birds.
We eat lunch.
We like the beach.

Pearson Education Limited
KAO Two
KAO Park, Harlow,
Essex, CMI7 9NA, England
and Associated Companies throughout the world.

ISBN: 978-1-2923- 4667-0

This edition first published by Pearson Education Ltd 2020

9 10 8

Set in Heinemann Roman Special, 19pt/28pt
Printed by Neografia, Slovakia

Published by Pearson Education Limited

Acknowledgments
123RF.com: kazoka30 18, Tatiana Atamaniuk 18
Getty Images: DigitalVision/Jose Luis Pelaez Inc 21, yulkapopkova 20-21
Shutterstock.com: Elena Sherengovskaya 21, SingjaiStock 17, Yarygin 16

For a complete list of the titles available in the Pearson English Readers series, visit www.pearsonenglishreaders.com.

Alternatively, write to your local Pearson Education office or to Pearson English Readers Marketing Department, Pearson Education, KAO Two, KAO Park, Harlow, Essex, CMI7 9NA